Duck Hunting Journal

- Field Notes -

Name

Contact Info

Year

Volume

"Immerse yourself in the outdoor experience. It will cleanse your soul and make you a better person."

Fred Bear

Copyright © 2020 Joseph F. Classen/Wild Revelation Outdoors

All rights reserved. No part of this written or photographic publication may be reproduced, stored in a retrieval system or transmitted in any form or by any means without the prior written permission of the publisher.

ISBN-13: 978-1-6514-5814-3

Wild Revelation Outdoors
www.wildrevelation.com

Duck Hunting Journal – Field Notes

Duck Hunting Journal – Field Notes

Date: _____

Location: _____

Weather Conditions: _____

Time Duration: _____

Hunt Party (& Dogs): _____

Service Providers: _____

Species	# Taken	# Lost	Male/Female
			/
			/
			/
			/
			/
Daily Totals			/

Gear Highlights/Comments:

_____

_____

_____

_____

Hunt Highlights/Comments:

_____

_____

_____

_____

_____

Miscellaneous Notes:

Duck Hunting Journal – Field Notes

Date: _____

Location: _____

Weather Conditions: _____

Time Duration: _____

Hunt Party (& Dogs): _____

Service Providers: _____

Species	# Taken	# Lost	Male/Female
			/
			/
			/
			/
			/
Daily Totals			/

Gear Highlights/Comments:

_____

_____

_____

Hunt Highlights/Comments:

_____

_____

_____

_____

Miscellaneous Notes:

Duck Hunting Journal – Field Notes

Date: _____

Location: _____

Weather Conditions: _____

Time Duration: _____

Hunt Party (& Dogs): _____

Service Providers: _____

Species	# Taken	# Lost	Male/Female
			/
			/
			/
			/
			/
Daily Totals			/

Gear Highlights/Comments:

_____

_____

_____

_____

Hunt Highlights/Comments:

_____

_____

_____

_____

_____

Miscellaneous Notes:

Duck Hunting Journal – Field Notes

Date: _____

Location: _____

Weather Conditions: _____

Time Duration: _____

Hunt Party (& Dogs): _____

Service Providers: _____

Species	# Taken	# Lost	Male/Female
			/
			/
			/
			/
			/
Daily Totals			/

Gear Highlights/Comments:

_____

_____

_____

_____

Hunt Highlights/Comments:

_____

_____

_____

_____

_____

Miscellaneous Notes:

Duck Hunting Journal – Field Notes

Date: _____

Location: _____

Weather Conditions: _____

Time Duration: _____

Hunt Party (& Dogs): _____

Service Providers: _____

Species	# Taken	# Lost	Male/Female
			/
			/
			/
			/
			/
Daily Totals			/

Gear Highlights/Comments:

_____

_____

_____

_____

Hunt Highlights/Comments:

_____

_____

_____

_____

_____

Miscellaneous Notes:

Duck Hunting Journal – Field Notes

Date: _____

Location: _____

Weather Conditions: _____

Time Duration: _____

Hunt Party (& Dogs): _____

Service Providers: _____

Species	# Taken	# Lost	Male/Female
			/
			/
			/
			/
			/
Daily Totals			/

Gear Highlights/Comments:

_____

_____

_____

_____

Hunt Highlights/Comments:

_____

_____

_____

_____

_____

Miscellaneous Notes:

Duck Hunting Journal – Field Notes

Date: _____

Location: _____

Weather Conditions: _____

Time Duration: _____

Hunt Party (& Dogs): _____

Service Providers: _____

Species	# Taken	# Lost	Male/Female
			/
			/
			/
			/
			/
Daily Totals			/

Gear Highlights/Comments:

_____

_____

_____

_____

Hunt Highlights/Comments:

_____

_____

_____

_____

_____

Miscellaneous Notes:

Duck Hunting Journal – Field Notes

Date: _____

Location: _____

Weather Conditions: _____

Time Duration: _____

Hunt Party (& Dogs): _____

Service Providers: _____

Species	# Taken	# Lost	Male/Female
			/
			/
			/
			/
			/
Daily Totals			/

Gear Highlights/Comments:

_____
_____
_____
_____

Hunt Highlights/Comments:

_____
_____
_____
_____
_____

Miscellaneous Notes:

Duck Hunting Journal – Field Notes

Date: _____

Location: _____

Weather Conditions: _____

Time Duration: _____

Hunt Party (& Dogs): _____

Service Providers: _____

Species	# Taken	# Lost	Male/Female
			/
			/
			/
			/
			/
Daily Totals			/

Gear Highlights/Comments:
_____
_____
_____
_____

Hunt Highlights/Comments:
_____
_____
_____
_____
_____

Miscellaneous Notes:

Duck Hunting Journal – Field Notes

Date: _____

Location: _____

Weather Conditions: _____

Time Duration: _____

Hunt Party (& Dogs): _____

Service Providers: _____

Species	# Taken	# Lost	Male/Female
			/
			/
			/
			/
			/
Daily Totals			/

Gear Highlights/Comments:

_____
_____
_____
_____

Hunt Highlights/Comments:

_____
_____
_____
_____
_____

Miscellaneous Notes:

Duck Hunting Journal – Field Notes

Date: _____

Location: _____

Weather Conditions: _____

Time Duration: _____

Hunt Party (& Dogs): _____

Service Providers: _____

Species	# Taken	# Lost	Male/Female
			/
			/
			/
			/
			/
Daily Totals			/

Gear Highlights/Comments:

_____

_____

_____

Hunt Highlights/Comments:

_____

_____

_____

_____

Miscellaneous Notes:

Duck Hunting Journal – Field Notes

Date: _____

Location: _____

Weather Conditions: _____

Time Duration: _____

Hunt Party (& Dogs): _____

Service Providers: _____

Species	# Taken	# Lost	Male/Female
			/
			/
			/
			/
			/
Daily Totals			/

Gear Highlights/Comments:

_____

_____

_____

_____

Hunt Highlights/Comments:

_____

_____

_____

_____

_____

Miscellaneous Notes:

Duck Hunting Journal – Field Notes

Date: _____

Location: _____

Weather Conditions: _____

Time Duration: _____

Hunt Party (& Dogs): _____

Service Providers: _____

Species	# Taken	# Lost	Male/Female
			/
			/
			/
			/
			/
Daily Totals			/

Gear Highlights/Comments:

_____
_____
_____
_____

Hunt Highlights/Comments:

_____
_____
_____
_____
_____

Miscellaneous Notes:

Duck Hunting Journal – Field Notes

Date: _____

Location: _____

Weather Conditions: _____

Time Duration: _____

Hunt Party (& Dogs): _____

Service Providers: _____

Species	# Taken	# Lost	Male/Female
			/
			/
			/
			/
			/
Daily Totals			/

Gear Highlights/Comments:

_____

_____

_____

_____

Hunt Highlights/Comments:

_____

_____

_____

_____

_____

Miscellaneous Notes:

Duck Hunting Journal – Field Notes

Date: _____

Location: _____

Weather Conditions: _____

Time Duration: _____

Hunt Party (& Dogs): _____

Service Providers: _____

Species	# Taken	# Lost	Male/Female
			/
			/
			/
			/
			/
Daily Totals			/

Gear Highlights/Comments:

_____

_____

_____

Hunt Highlights/Comments:

_____

_____

_____

_____

Miscellaneous Notes:

Duck Hunting Journal – Field Notes

Date: _____

Location: _____

Weather Conditions: _____

Time Duration: _____

Hunt Party (& Dogs): _____

Service Providers: _____

Species	# Taken	# Lost	Male/Female
			/
			/
			/
			/
			/
Daily Totals			/

Gear Highlights/Comments:

_____

_____

_____

_____

Hunt Highlights/Comments:

_____

_____

_____

_____

_____

Miscellaneous Notes:

Duck Hunting Journal – Field Notes

Date: _____

Location: _____

Weather Conditions: _____

Time Duration: _____

Hunt Party (& Dogs): _____

Service Providers: _____

Species	# Taken	# Lost	Male/Female
			/
			/
			/
			/
			/
Daily Totals			/

Gear Highlights/Comments:

_____
_____
_____

Hunt Highlights/Comments:

_____
_____
_____
_____
_____

Miscellaneous Notes:

Duck Hunting Journal – Field Notes

Date: _____

Location: _____

Weather Conditions: _____

Time Duration: _____

Hunt Party (& Dogs): _____

Service Providers: _____

Species	# Taken	# Lost	Male/Female
			/
			/
			/
			/
			/
Daily Totals			/

Gear Highlights/Comments:

_____

_____

_____

Hunt Highlights/Comments:

_____

_____

_____

_____

Miscellaneous Notes:

Duck Hunting Journal – Field Notes

Date: _____

Location: _____

Weather Conditions: _____

Time Duration: _____

Hunt Party (& Dogs): _____

Service Providers: _____

Species	# Taken	# Lost	Male/Female
			/
			/
			/
			/
			/
Daily Totals			/

Gear Highlights/Comments:

_____

_____

_____

_____

Hunt Highlights/Comments:

_____

_____

_____

_____

_____

Miscellaneous Notes:

Date: _____

Location: _____

Weather Conditions: _____

Time Duration: _____

Hunt Party (& Dogs): _____

Service Providers: _____

Species	# Taken	# Lost	Male/Female
			/
			/
			/
			/
			/
Daily Totals			/

Gear Highlights/Comments:

_____
_____
_____
_____

Hunt Highlights/Comments:

_____
_____
_____
_____
_____

Miscellaneous Notes:

Duck Hunting Journal – Field Notes

Date: _____

Location: _____

Weather Conditions: _____

Time Duration: _____

Hunt Party (& Dogs): _____

Service Providers: _____

Species	# Taken	# Lost	Male/Female
			/
			/
			/
			/
			/
Daily Totals			/

Gear Highlights/Comments:
_____
_____
_____
_____

Hunt Highlights/Comments:
_____
_____
_____
_____
_____

Miscellaneous Notes:

Duck Hunting Journal – Field Notes

Date: _____

Location: _____

Weather Conditions: _____

Time Duration: _____

Hunt Party (& Dogs): _____

Service Providers: _____

Species	# Taken	# Lost	Male/Female
			/
			/
			/
			/
			/
Daily Totals			/

Gear Highlights/Comments:

_____

_____

_____

_____

Hunt Highlights/Comments:

_____

_____

_____

_____

Miscellaneous Notes:

Duck Hunting Journal – Field Notes

Date: _____

Location: _____

Weather Conditions: _____

Time Duration: _____

Hunt Party (& Dogs): _____

Service Providers: _____

Species	# Taken	# Lost	Male/Female
			/
			/
			/
			/
			/
Daily Totals			/

Gear Highlights/Comments:

_____

_____

_____

_____

Hunt Highlights/Comments:

_____

_____

_____

_____

_____

_____

Miscellaneous Notes:

Duck Hunting Journal – Field Notes

Date: _____

Location: _____

Weather Conditions: _____

Time Duration: _____

Hunt Party (& Dogs): _____

Service Providers: _____

Species	# Taken	# Lost	Male/Female
			/
			/
			/
			/
			/
Daily Totals			/

Gear Highlights/Comments:

_____

_____

_____

Hunt Highlights/Comments:

_____

_____

_____

_____

Miscellaneous Notes:

Duck Hunting Journal – Field Notes

Date: _____

Location: _____

Weather Conditions: _____

Time Duration: _____

Hunt Party (& Dogs): _____

Service Providers: _____

Species	# Taken	# Lost	Male/Female
			/
			/
			/
			/
			/
Daily Totals			/

Gear Highlights/Comments:

_____
_____
_____

Hunt Highlights/Comments:

_____
_____
_____
_____
_____

Miscellaneous Notes:

Duck Hunting Journal – Field Notes

Date: _____

Location: _____

Weather Conditions: _____

Time Duration: _____

Hunt Party (& Dogs): _____

Service Providers: _____

Species	# Taken	# Lost	Male/Female
			/
			/
			/
			/
			/
Daily Totals			/

Gear Highlights/Comments:

_____
_____
_____
_____

Hunt Highlights/Comments:

_____
_____
_____
_____
_____

Miscellaneous Notes:

Duck Hunting Journal – Field Notes

Date: _____

Location: _____

Weather Conditions: _____

Time Duration: _____

Hunt Party (& Dogs): _____

Service Providers: _____

Species	# Taken	# Lost	Male/Female
			/
			/
			/
			/
			/
Daily Totals			/

Gear Highlights/Comments:

_____
_____
_____
_____

Hunt Highlights/Comments:

_____
_____
_____
_____
_____
_____

Miscellaneous Notes:

Duck Hunting Journal – Field Notes

Date: _____

Location: _____

Weather Conditions: _____

Time Duration: _____

Hunt Party (& Dogs): _____

Service Providers: _____

Species	# Taken	# Lost	Male/Female
			/
			/
			/
			/
			/
Daily Totals			/

Gear Highlights/Comments:

_____

_____

_____

_____

Hunt Highlights/Comments:

_____

_____

_____

_____

_____

Miscellaneous Notes:

Duck Hunting Journal – Field Notes

Date: _____

Location: _____

Weather Conditions: _____

Time Duration: _____

Hunt Party (& Dogs): _____

Service Providers: _____

Species	# Taken	# Lost	Male/Female
			/
			/
			/
			/
			/
Daily Totals			/

Gear Highlights/Comments:

_____
_____
_____
_____

Hunt Highlights/Comments:

_____
_____
_____
_____
_____

Miscellaneous Notes:

Duck Hunting Journal – Field Notes

Date: _____

Location: _____

Weather Conditions: _____

Time Duration: _____

Hunt Party (& Dogs): _____

Service Providers: _____

Species	# Taken	# Lost	Male/Female
			/
			/
			/
			/
			/
Daily Totals			/

Gear Highlights/Comments:

_____

_____

_____

Hunt Highlights/Comments:

_____

_____

_____

_____

Miscellaneous Notes:

Duck Hunting Journal – Field Notes

Date: _____

Location: _____

Weather Conditions: _____

Time Duration: _____

Hunt Party (& Dogs): _____

Service Providers: _____

Species	# Taken	# Lost	Male/Female
			/
			/
			/
			/
			/
Daily Totals			/

Gear Highlights/Comments:

_____

_____

_____

_____

Hunt Highlights/Comments:

_____

_____

_____

_____

_____

Miscellaneous Notes:

Duck Hunting Journal – Field Notes

Date: _____

Location: _____

Weather Conditions: _____

Time Duration: _____

Hunt Party (& Dogs): _____

Service Providers: _____

Species	# Taken	# Lost	Male/Female
			/
			/
			/
			/
			/
Daily Totals			/

Gear Highlights/Comments:

_____
_____
_____
_____

Hunt Highlights/Comments:

_____
_____
_____
_____
_____

Miscellaneous Notes:

Duck Hunting Journal – Field Notes

Date: _____

Location: _____

Weather Conditions: _____

Time Duration: _____

Hunt Party (& Dogs): _____

Service Providers: _____

Species	# Taken	# Lost	Male/Female
			/
			/
			/
			/
			/
Daily Totals			/

Gear Highlights/Comments:

_____

_____

_____

_____

Hunt Highlights/Comments:

_____

_____

_____

_____

_____

Miscellaneous Notes:

Duck Hunting Journal – Field Notes

Date: _____

Location: _____

Weather Conditions: _____

Time Duration: _____

Hunt Party (& Dogs): _____

Service Providers: _____

Species	# Taken	# Lost	Male/Female
			/
			/
			/
			/
			/
Daily Totals			/

Gear Highlights/Comments:

_____

_____

_____

_____

Hunt Highlights/Comments:

_____

_____

_____

_____

_____

Miscellaneous Notes:

Duck Hunting Journal – Field Notes

Date: _____

Location: _____

Weather Conditions: _____

Time Duration: _____

Hunt Party (& Dogs): _____

Service Providers: _____

Species	# Taken	# Lost	Male/Female
			/
			/
			/
			/
			/
Daily Totals			/

Gear Highlights/Comments:

_____

_____

_____

_____

Hunt Highlights/Comments:

_____

_____

_____

_____

Miscellaneous Notes:

Duck Hunting Journal – Field Notes

Date: _____

Location: _____

Weather Conditions: _____

Time Duration: _____

Hunt Party (& Dogs): _____

Service Providers: _____

Species	# Taken	# Lost	Male/Female
			/
			/
			/
			/
			/
Daily Totals			/

Gear Highlights/Comments:

_____
_____
_____
_____

Hunt Highlights/Comments:

_____
_____
_____
_____
_____

Miscellaneous Notes:

Duck Hunting Journal – Field Notes

Date: _____

Location: _____

Weather Conditions: _____

Time Duration: _____

Hunt Party (& Dogs): _____

Service Providers: _____

Species	# Taken	# Lost	Male/Female
			/
			/
			/
			/
			/
Daily Totals			/

Gear Highlights/Comments:

_____

_____

_____

_____

Hunt Highlights/Comments:

_____

_____

_____

_____

_____

Miscellaneous Notes:

Duck Hunting Journal – Field Notes

Date: _____

Location: _____

Weather Conditions: _____

Time Duration: _____

Hunt Party (& Dogs): _____

Service Providers: _____

Species	# Taken	# Lost	Male/Female
			/
			/
			/
			/
			/
Daily Totals			/

Gear Highlights/Comments:

_____

_____

_____

_____

Hunt Highlights/Comments:

_____

_____

_____

_____

Miscellaneous Notes:

Duck Hunting Journal – Field Notes

Date: _____

Location: _____

Weather Conditions: _____

Time Duration: _____

Hunt Party (& Dogs): _____

Service Providers: _____

Species	# Taken	# Lost	Male/Female
			/
			/
			/
			/
			/
Daily Totals			/

Gear Highlights/Comments:

_____

_____

_____

_____

Hunt Highlights/Comments:

_____

_____

_____

_____

_____

Miscellaneous Notes:

Duck Hunting Journal – Field Notes

Date: _____

Location: _____

Weather Conditions: _____

Time Duration: _____

Hunt Party (& Dogs): _____

Service Providers: _____

Species	# Taken	# Lost	Male/Female
			/
			/
			/
			/
			/
Daily Totals			/

Gear Highlights/Comments:

_____

_____

_____

_____

Hunt Highlights/Comments:

_____

_____

_____

_____

_____

Miscellaneous Notes:

Duck Hunting Journal – Field Notes

Date: _____

Location: _____

Weather Conditions: _____

Time Duration: _____

Hunt Party (& Dogs): _____

Service Providers: _____

Species	# Taken	# Lost	Male/Female
			/
			/
			/
			/
			/
Daily Totals			/

Gear Highlights/Comments:

_____

_____

_____

_____

Hunt Highlights/Comments:

_____

_____

_____

_____

Miscellaneous Notes:

Duck Hunting Journal – Field Notes

Date: _____

Location: _____

Weather Conditions: _____

Time Duration: _____

Hunt Party (& Dogs): _____

Service Providers: _____

Species	# Taken	# Lost	Male/Female
			/
			/
			/
			/
			/
Daily Totals			/

Gear Highlights/Comments:

_____

_____

_____

_____

Hunt Highlights/Comments:

_____

_____

_____

_____

Miscellaneous Notes:

Duck Hunting Journal – Field Notes

Date: _____

Location: _____

Weather Conditions: _____

Time Duration: _____

Hunt Party (& Dogs): _____

Service Providers: _____

Species	# Taken	# Lost	Male/Female
			/
			/
			/
			/
			/
Daily Totals			/

Gear Highlights/Comments:

_____

_____

_____

Hunt Highlights/Comments:

_____

_____

_____

_____

Miscellaneous Notes:

Duck Hunting Journal – Field Notes

Date: _____

Location: _____

Weather Conditions: _____

Time Duration: _____

Hunt Party (& Dogs): _____

Service Providers: _____

Species	# Taken	# Lost	Male/Female
			/
			/
			/
			/
			/
Daily Totals			/

Gear Highlights/Comments:

_____
_____
_____
_____

Hunt Highlights/Comments:

_____
_____
_____
_____
_____

Miscellaneous Notes:

Duck Hunting Journal – Field Notes

Date: _____

Location: _____

Weather Conditions: _____

Time Duration: _____

Hunt Party (& Dogs): _____

Service Providers: _____

Species	# Taken	# Lost	Male/Female
			/
			/
			/
			/
			/
Daily Totals			/

Gear Highlights/Comments:

_____

_____

_____

_____

Hunt Highlights/Comments:

_____

_____

_____

_____

_____

Miscellaneous Notes:

Duck Hunting Journal – Field Notes

Date: _____

Location: _____

Weather Conditions: _____

Time Duration: _____

Hunt Party (& Dogs): _____

Service Providers: _____

Species	# Taken	# Lost	Male/Female
			/
			/
			/
			/
			/
Daily Totals			/

Gear Highlights/Comments:

_____

_____

_____

_____

Hunt Highlights/Comments:

_____

_____

_____

_____

Miscellaneous Notes:

Duck Hunting Journal – Field Notes

Date: _____

Location: _____

Weather Conditions: _____

Time Duration: _____

Hunt Party (& Dogs): _____

Service Providers: _____

Species	# Taken	# Lost	Male/Female
			/
			/
			/
			/
			/
Daily Totals			/

Gear Highlights/Comments:

_____

_____

_____

Hunt Highlights/Comments:

_____

_____

_____

_____

Miscellaneous Notes:

Date: _____

Location: _____

Weather Conditions: _____

Time Duration: _____

Hunt Party (& Dogs): _____

Service Providers: _____

Species	# Taken	# Lost	Male/Female
			/
			/
			/
			/
			/
Daily Totals			/

Gear Highlights/Comments:

_____

_____

_____

_____

Hunt Highlights/Comments:

_____

_____

_____

_____

Miscellaneous Notes:

Duck Hunting Journal – Field Notes

Date: _____

Location: _____

Weather Conditions: _____

Time Duration: _____

Hunt Party (& Dogs): _____

Service Providers: _____

Species	# Taken	# Lost	Male/Female
			/
			/
			/
			/
			/
Daily Totals			/

Gear Highlights/Comments:

_____

_____

_____

_____

Hunt Highlights/Comments:

_____

_____

_____

_____

_____

Miscellaneous Notes:

Duck Hunting Journal – Field Notes

Date: _____

Location: _____

Weather Conditions: _____

Time Duration: _____

Hunt Party (& Dogs): _____

Service Providers: _____

Species	# Taken	# Lost	Male/Female
			/
			/
			/
			/
			/
Daily Totals			/

Gear Highlights/Comments:

_____
_____
_____

Hunt Highlights/Comments:

_____
_____
_____
_____

Miscellaneous Notes:

Duck Hunting Journal – Field Notes

Date: _____

Location: _____

Weather Conditions: _____

Time Duration: _____

Hunt Party (& Dogs): _____

Service Providers: _____

Species	# Taken	# Lost	Male/Female
			/
			/
			/
			/
			/
Daily Totals			/

Gear Highlights/Comments:

_____

_____

_____

_____

Hunt Highlights/Comments:

_____

_____

_____

_____

Miscellaneous Notes:

Duck Hunting Journal – Field Notes

Date: _____

Location: _____

Weather Conditions: _____

Time Duration: _____

Hunt Party (& Dogs): _____

Service Providers: _____

Species	# Taken	# Lost	Male/Female
			/
			/
			/
			/
			/
Daily Totals			/

Gear Highlights/Comments:

_____

_____

_____

Hunt Highlights/Comments:

_____

_____

_____

_____

Miscellaneous Notes:

Duck Hunting Journal – Field Notes

Date: _____

Location: _____

Weather Conditions: _____

Time Duration: _____

Hunt Party (& Dogs): _____

Service Providers: _____

Species	# Taken	# Lost	Male/Female
			/
			/
			/
			/
			/
Daily Totals			/

Gear Highlights/Comments:

_____

_____

_____

_____

Hunt Highlights/Comments:

_____

_____

_____

_____

_____

Miscellaneous Notes:

Duck Hunting Journal – Field Notes

Date: _____

Location: _____

Weather Conditions: _____

Time Duration: _____

Hunt Party (& Dogs): _____

Service Providers: _____

Species	# Taken	# Lost	Male/Female
			/
			/
			/
			/
			/
Daily Totals			/

Gear Highlights/Comments:

_____
_____
_____
_____

Hunt Highlights/Comments:

_____
_____
_____
_____
_____

Miscellaneous Notes:

Date: _____

Location: _____

Weather Conditions: _____

Time Duration: _____

Hunt Party (& Dogs): _____

Service Providers: _____

Species	# Taken	# Lost	Male/Female
			/
			/
			/
			/
			/
Daily Totals			/

Gear Highlights/Comments:

_____

_____

_____

_____

Hunt Highlights/Comments:

_____

_____

_____

_____

Miscellaneous Notes:

Duck Hunting Journal – Field Notes

Date: _____

Location: _____

Weather Conditions: _____

Time Duration: _____

Hunt Party (& Dogs): _____

Service Providers: _____

Species	# Taken	# Lost	Male/Female
			/
			/
			/
			/
			/
Daily Totals			/

Gear Highlights/Comments:

_____

_____

_____

_____

Hunt Highlights/Comments:

_____

_____

_____

_____

_____

Miscellaneous Notes:

Duck Hunting Journal – Field Notes

Date: _____

Location: _____

Weather Conditions: _____

Time Duration: _____

Hunt Party (& Dogs): _____

Service Providers: _____

Species	# Taken	# Lost	Male/Female
			/
			/
			/
			/
			/
Daily Totals			/

Gear Highlights/Comments:

_____

_____

_____

_____

Hunt Highlights/Comments:

_____

_____

_____

_____

Miscellaneous Notes:

Duck Hunting Journal – Field Notes

Date: _____

Location: _____

Weather Conditions: _____

Time Duration: _____

Hunt Party (& Dogs): _____

Service Providers: _____

Species	# Taken	# Lost	Male/Female
			/
			/
			/
			/
			/
Daily Totals			/

Gear Highlights/Comments:

_____

_____

_____

_____

Hunt Highlights/Comments:

_____

_____

_____

_____

_____

Miscellaneous Notes:

Date: _____

Location: _____

Weather Conditions: _____

Time Duration: _____

Hunt Party (& Dogs): _____

Service Providers: _____

Species	# Taken	# Lost	Male/Female
			/
			/
			/
			/
			/
Daily Totals			/

Gear Highlights/Comments:

_____

_____

_____

_____

Hunt Highlights/Comments:

_____

_____

_____

_____

Miscellaneous Notes:

Duck Hunting Journal – Field Notes

Date: _____

Location: _____

Weather Conditions: _____

Time Duration: _____

Hunt Party (& Dogs): _____

Service Providers: _____

Species	# Taken	# Lost	Male/Female
			/
			/
			/
			/
			/
Daily Totals			/

Gear Highlights/Comments:

_____

_____

_____

Hunt Highlights/Comments:

_____

_____

_____

_____

Miscellaneous Notes:

Duck Hunting Journal – Field Notes

Date: _____

Location: _____

Weather Conditions: _____

Time Duration: _____

Hunt Party (& Dogs): _____

Service Providers: _____

Species	# Taken	# Lost	Male/Female
			/
			/
			/
			/
			/
Daily Totals			/

Gear Highlights/Comments:

_____

_____

_____

_____

Hunt Highlights/Comments:

_____

_____

_____

_____

Miscellaneous Notes:

Duck Hunting Journal – Field Notes

Date: _____

Location: _____

Weather Conditions: _____

Time Duration: _____

Hunt Party (& Dogs): _____

Service Providers: _____

Species	# Taken	# Lost	Male/Female
			/
			/
			/
			/
			/
Daily Totals			/

Gear Highlights/Comments:

_____

_____

_____

Hunt Highlights/Comments:

_____

_____

_____

_____

Miscellaneous Notes:

Duck Hunting Journal – Field Notes

Date: _____

Location: _____

Weather Conditions: _____

Time Duration: _____

Hunt Party (& Dogs): _____

Service Providers: _____

Species	# Taken	# Lost	Male/Female
			/
			/
			/
			/
			/
Daily Totals			/

Gear Highlights/Comments:

_____

_____

_____

Hunt Highlights/Comments:

_____

_____

_____

_____

Miscellaneous Notes:

Duck Hunting Journal – Field Notes

Date: _____

Location: _____

Weather Conditions: _____

Time Duration: _____

Hunt Party (& Dogs): _____

Service Providers: _____

Species	# Taken	# Lost	Male/Female
			/
			/
			/
			/
			/
Daily Totals			/

Gear Highlights/Comments:

_____

_____

_____

_____

Hunt Highlights/Comments:

_____

_____

_____

_____

_____

Miscellaneous Notes:

Duck Hunting Journal – Field Notes

Date: _____

Location: _____

Weather Conditions: _____

Time Duration: _____

Hunt Party (& Dogs): _____

Service Providers: _____

Species	# Taken	# Lost	Male/Female
			/
			/
			/
			/
			/
Daily Totals			/

Gear Highlights/Comments:

_____
_____
_____
_____

Hunt Highlights/Comments:

_____
_____
_____
_____
_____

Miscellaneous Notes:

Duck Hunting Journal – Field Notes

Date: _____

Location: _____

Weather Conditions: _____

Time Duration: _____

Hunt Party (& Dogs): _____

Service Providers: _____

Species	# Taken	# Lost	Male/Female
			/
			/
			/
			/
			/
Daily Totals			/

Gear Highlights/Comments:

_____
_____
_____
_____

Hunt Highlights/Comments:

_____
_____
_____
_____
_____

Miscellaneous Notes:

Duck Hunting Journal – Field Notes

Date: _____

Location: _____

Weather Conditions: _____

Time Duration: _____

Hunt Party (& Dogs): _____

Service Providers: _____

Species	# Taken	# Lost	Male/Female
			/
			/
			/
			/
			/
Daily Totals			/

Gear Highlights/Comments:

_____
_____
_____
_____

Hunt Highlights/Comments:

_____
_____
_____
_____

Miscellaneous Notes:

Get Extra Copies to Build your Personal Hunting Journal Library.

Order additional copies at Amazon.com or Wild Revelation Outdoors

Don't Miss Out on All the Adventure!

Wild Revelation Outdoors produces a wide variety of entertaining, educational, and inspirational multimedia, as well as operates an Alaskan guide and adventure/travel consultation service. Additionally, we feature an online Amazon affiliate store where one can shop *exclusively* for the most dependable, highest quality outdoor products on the market from the most reliable, proven brands in the world.

Visit us today at www.wildrevelation.com

Thank You!

Thank you for purchasing this book. We are extremely grateful. If you enjoyed this book, we'd like to hear from you and hope that you could take some time to post an honest review on Amazon. Your feedback and support will help *Wild Revelation Outdoors Publishing* to improve the quality of our products for the future.

Made in the USA
Columbia, SC
03 March 2020